NEW ENGLAND

A PICTORIAL SOUVENIR

CAROL M. HIGHSMITH AND TED LANDPHAIR

NEW ENGLAND

A PICTORIAL SOUVENIR

CRESCENT BOOKS

NEW YORK

PAGES 2–3: *The
picturesque little town
of Barnet, Vermont,
with its requisite
steepled white church,
prompts a stop along
Interstate 91 for
a quintessential
fall New England
photograph.*
PAGES 6–7: *Sheep
once grazed on the
Boston Common,
the point of reference
from which the
city's historic attrac-
tions and
office towers
are explored. The
Common and the
adjacent Public
Garden are jewels
in a string of green-
swards, pedestrian
malls, fens, and
parks called the
"Emerald Necklace."*

THE AUTHORS GRATEFULLY ACKNOWLEDGE
THE SERVICES, ACCOMMODATIONS, AND SUPPORT PROVIDED BY
HILTON HOTELS CORPORATION
IN CONNECTION WITH THE COMPLETION OF THIS BOOK.

————

*This 1997 edition is published by Crescent Books,
a division of Random House Value Publishing, Inc.,
201 East 50th Street, New York, NY 10022.*

*Crescent Books and colophon are trademarks of
Random House Value Publishing, Inc.*

*Random House
New York • Toronto • London • Sydney • Auckland
http://www.randomhouse.com/*

Printed and bound in China

*A CIP catalog record for this book is available from
the Library of Congress.*

ISBN 0-517-20145-3

8   7   6   5   4   3   2   1

————

Designed by Robert L. Wiser, Archetype Press, Inc., Washington, D.C.

FOREWORD

New England is America's most defined region. There can be lively debate about what constitutes the West or the South or the Mid-West. But there is no doubt about the six historic states—Connecticut, Rhode Island, Massachusetts, Maine, New Hampshire, and Vermont—that make up New England. One can live fifty feet across the Vermont line in New York and not be a New Englander, not possess the same independent ways or emotional attachment to the past. Named New England by Captain John Smith as he explored the Massachusetts coast in 1614, the area's first European settlers were guided by a stern religion that encouraged isolation and a deep respect for privacy. Indeed, the romantic notion of New England as a hardscrabble, pastoral haven of feisty individualists is truly rooted in reality and has been reinforced by an influx of outsiders—"emotional New Englanders"—who have brought even more zeal than some natives to the fight to retain the region's character.

Together, the region's six renowned states possess an arresting collective personality, yet each state retains a character and charm all its own. Massachusetts—where protests against British taxes and tariff would prompt boycotts of British goods, resulting in the "Boston Tea Party" and, ultimately, the American Revolution—is not only home to many of America's most important and exciting cultural landmarks, but is a highly urbanized and industrialized state as well. Connecticut, "The Constitution State," now a weekend and day-trippers' paradise, full of quaint inns, fabulous museums, and plenty of smooth sailing on the Long Island Sound, was settled by squatters, in 1639, on land bordering the Connecticut River. Drafting a document called the "Fundamental Orders," these pioneers established a government that can be viewed as the world's oldest autonomous, self-governing entity. Robert Frost once wrote, "It's restful just to think about New Hampshire." With its modest seashore, spectacular mountains, picturesque villages, covered bridges, old country homes, and small industries, New Hampshire is often voted America's most livable state. In Maine, lobstermen still fish the same backbreaking way their forefathers did. Winters are long; cabin fever runs high; and during spring's "mud season," newly thawed dirt roads are all but impassable. Yet, the state's prized lobster bakes, lighthouse tours, snowmobiling excursions, and moose-watching safaris draw visitors again and again. Vermont, land of rolling dairy farms, world-famous maple syrup, and the glorious Green Mountains, has been discovered by developers, tourists, enthusiastic new residents, and parents seeking summer camps for their children. And, finally, tiny Rhode Island, founded as a haven from religious persecution, boasts an Ivy League college (Brown) and some of the nation's most extravagant mansions, including The Breakers, the magnificent summer "cottage" of Cornelius Vanderbilt.

Today, although three-fourths of all New Englanders live in cities, and there are twelve times more white-collar professionals than farmers and fishermen combined, outlanders still come looking for the simple farmhouse, the lobsterman or the white, steepled Congregational church on the manicured green—images planted in the mind forever by artists like Norman Rockwell and Nathaniel Currier and James Merritt Ives. New England, it seems, is a state of mind.

I. M. Pei's shimmering John Hancock Tower (opposite) replaced the Custom House Tower as Boston's most recognizable architectural landmark, and its observation deck became a favorite city overlook. From the roof of an older, squatter Hancock Building nearby, observers with binoculars stood watch, looking for windowpanes in the new building that showed signs of shattering. So acute was the problem that each of the 10,344, five-hundred-pound "lights" of glass was eventually replaced. Dunster Hall's tower (left) looms above Harvard University, the nation's first college, in Cambridge. Down the road, at Harvard Square—which is not square at all but triangular—shops, banks, an international newsstand, and a subway station flank the great halls of learning. One, Widener Library, contains the nation's second largest collection of books.

Sir Henry Kitson's Minute Man statue— a likeness of Captain John Parker— stands on the edge of the Lexington, Massachusetts, green, where seventy-seven citizen-soldiers first encountered the force of seven hundred British troops sent from Boston ("two if by sea") to search out the colonists' suspected cache of arms. Captain Parker's orders— "Stand your ground; don't fire unless fired upon, but if they mean to have war, let it begin here"— are engraved on a boulder near the statue. Eight Minute Men, but no British soldiers, died in the skirmish, after which the British marched to their intended destination a few miles down the road in Concord. The remains of American patriots who fell at Lexington are buried in a modest graveyard on the Lexington green. Lexington citizens often dress as colonists or British troops and officers (above) for visiting groups of schoolchildren.

Lowell's Boott Cotton Mill No. 6, now a National Park Service monument to the Industrial Revolution, was a hub of activity for almost a century until it closed, like so many others in New England in the 1950s and '60s. The work on the looms involved threading the machines, checking fibers constantly to be sure they did not twist or break, and changing bobbins and shuttles—and was dangerous and deafening. Boott's bell (opposite) summoned the young "Lowell girls," many of whom worked long hours to send their earnings home to families on hardscrabble farms. From her chaperoned apartment, one girl wrote in 1889 that the weave room's cacophony "could not drown the music of my thoughts."

The 1765 Knowles-Doane House (right) near Eastham on Cape Cod is a classic "half-Cape" cottage, meaning there are two windows to one side of the front door and none on the other. (In a full Cape cottage, there are two windows on each side.) This part of Cape Cod, away from the busy towns close to the Massachusetts mainland, is full of picturesque lanes, artists' cabins—and even wildlife, including coyotes. The Cape also features virtually uninterrupted beaches and a national seashore full of wild and shifting dunes. Offshore on Nantucket Island, cottages take different shapes. Most are clad in uniform gray shingles, in keeping with the island's rigid architectural dictates, but many, like this one (above) in Siasconset, sport colorful flower boxes.

Sunlovers like Kristan Palmer of Sudbury, Massachusetts, appreciate the pristine beaches of Nantucket Island (opposite). Nantucket town itself had turned decrepit as the island's whaling industry declined. Revitalized, it is now home port to some of the fanciest yachts in the Northeast, and downtown became a tourist mecca after it added eclectic shops and epicurean restaurants. And Nantucket retains several lighthouses (right) and other charms. The island's growing concern is the tide of automobiles, carried by ferry from the mainland.
OVERLEAF: Old Sturbridge Village is an "outdoor museum" of authentic early-nineteenth-century buildings moved to central Massachusetts. Museum staff in period clothing farm the fields and gardens and lead visitors through chores and demonstrations in the farm fields and more than forty restored buildings.

Like many of the other higher elevations in New England, the Berkshire Mountains (left and above) in Massachusetts burst into glorious color come fall, attracting legions of "leaf peepers." New England's red and sugar maples turn a deeper shade of red and orange than do trees in most other parts of the nation.

The orange and yellow are present all year long but are masked by green chlorophyll until autumn. The red is created by a separate hormone, stirred by the cold nights and warm days of fall. Eventually a heavy rain or stiff wind breaks leaves from branches and sends them swirling to the ground below.

Flags are fully furled on the whaleship Charles W. Morgan (left), one of more than 450 historic watercraft at Mystic Seaport, a nonprofit maritime museum along the Mystic River in Connecticut. Among the museum and research center's more than two million artifacts are several wooden ships' figureheads such as that from the Great Admiral *(above).*

Opposite: *The 1896 bronze statue of former university president Theodore Dwight Woolsey sits before the entrance of Dwight Hall— the former college library now used as a volunteer center— on Yale University's Old Campus in New Haven. Chartered in 1701 as "The Collegiate School," Yale is a cornerstone of the New Haven, Connecticut, economy.*

A bit of downtown in America's "Insurance City," Hartford, Connecticut, peeks over the trees above the 1899 Corning Fountain (left) in Bushnell Park. John J. Corning of New York commissioned the fountain in memory of his father, a Hartford merchant. Its statues recall the area's original Saukiog Indians, and the hart atop the fountain symbolizes the white settlers of the city from Herefordshire, England. Architect Richard Upjohn of New York horrified Hartford when he topped the new state capitol (opposite) with a Tuscan clock tower rather than the customary dome in 1872. A winged statue called the "Genius of Connecticut" once stood atop the dome, but it was found to be insecurely mounted following a rare hurricane in 1938 and was removed. During World War II, the statue was melted for scrap metal.

The double overhang, brownstone steps, bootscraper, and original front door and hinges of the pre-Revolutionary Huntington Tavern (above), once the finest house and hostel on the Norwich, Connecticut, green, caught Stephen Mack's eye. Mack rescues doomed historic houses, disassembling them after photographing each piece, storing the components at his farm in Ashaway, Rhode Island, then reassembling the structures for clients in other locales. Or, as in the case of Huntington Tavern, he will use a board here, a sconce there, to make another old property whole. "It's like an organ transplant," he says. "Never from a living donor." He took the walls in the north bedchamber (right) down to their 1768 surface, leaving a mottled veneer on the original wood paneling.

In 1846, Henry Chandler Bowen, a prosperous Brooklyn, New York, dry-goods merchant, built a summer home, Roseland Cottage & Ice House (above), in his birthplace of Woodstock in Connecticut's northeast "Quiet Corner." Most of the other fine houses in town were Gothic Revival style, associated with Christian piety. But Bowen, an amateur horticulturist, stunned his neighbors by borrowing a color from his formal parterre boxwood garden and painting Roseland a shocking pink—not once but thirteen different times during the fifty years he summered there. The house did have one sedate, sacred motif: stained-glass windows (opposite) in its parlors. Around Independence Day each year, Bowen threw the ultimate of all nineteenth-century parties for the whole town. It featured speeches, music, and an afternoon of croquet. Four sitting presidents—Ulysses Grant, Rutherford Hayes, Benjamin Harrison, and William McKinley—made the scene.

Rhode Island's white Georgian-marble statehouse (above), one of America's most majestic capitols, overlooks downtown Providence from Constitution Hill. It features the second-largest self-supporting dome in the world. Only that of Saint Peter's Basilica in Rome is larger. RIGHT: The Modern Diner in Pawtucket, Rhode Island, is a "Sterling Streamliner"—"Car No. 4140"—built in 1940 by the Judkins Company of Massachusetts as the latest racy aero-dynamic model in its line of "sisters to Streamliners of rail and air." On Thursdays especially—payday in blue-collar Pawtucket—the Modern Diner was the "place to be," but fast-food restaurants put it out of business for six years until Anthony Demou and his brother-in-law rescued, moved, and reopened the diner in 1983.

Rose Island Lighthouse (above) off Newport, Rhode Island, is more properly called a light station, since it had a keeper (and family). Built in 1869, it sent out a steady red beacon until 1971, when the U.S. Coast Guard closed it after guiding lights were installed in a new bay bridge. (Not all lighthouses give off oscillating white beams; Rose Island's steady red was one of a series of signals that gave mariners their bearings.) The lighthouse changed hands several times until the city purchased it in 1985 for $2,300 and turned it over to a nonprofit foundation that renovated it and now operates it as an unusual museum and hostel— unusual because guests participate in an ecological adventure, composting, cleaning the beach, and carefully monitoring their electricity and water use. Some visitors stay in the keeper's old bedroom (right).

New York Central Railroad President William K. Vanderbilt commissioned Richard Morris Hunt to design a Louis XIV–style summer home, Marble House, in Newport, Rhode Island, for his wife, Alva, in the early 1880s. Soon she would divorce him but keep Marble House. Guests were served meals beneath the dining room's gilt relief ceiling (left). Alva's teahouse (above), an example of American Chinoserie architecture on the city Cliff Walk, was a place to contemplate the beauty of nature and "refresh the heart." Mrs. Vanderbilt, an ardent woman's suffragist, dedicated the teahouse at a suffrage conference in 1914. Marble House's dining room (overleaf) was patterned after the Salon of Hercules at Versailles.

Portsmouth, New Hampshire's Strawbery Banke museum (right) features authentic Colonial-era neighborhoods, including these houses along Puddle Lane. Once the city's premier neighborhood, Strawbery Banke deteriorated into a slum before being rescued by nonprofit foundations. Along with their doses of colonialism, visitors are delighted to find twentieth-century Americana displays, including a 1950s kitchen (above). The 1817 Frye's Measure Mill (overleaf) in Wilton, New Hampshire, began as a "carding and fulling" operation, cleansing, disentangling (carding), and thickening (fulling) farmers' wool. Later, it turned out delicate maple and fruitwood boxes as well as simple dippers and other dry measures used when most goods were sold in bulk in bins at general stores.

At their benches at Frye's Measure Mill (above), craftsworkers made and repaired their own molds; bent and shaped thinly peeled, soaked wood into containers called measures (including dippers called "piggins"; and added pegs, brads, and handles. Even today, the work area is unheated. In New Hampshire's bitter wintertime, workers follow the warming sun from room to room and task to task. Today the mill is run by Harley Savage— who had studied oceanography and art but elected to join his father in business— and his wife, Pam. They're still making utilitarian measures and dippers but have added a line of beautiful Shaker and "pantry" boxes. "Restoration here is an everyday event," Savage says. "Our millwright is always crafting new parts in the machine shop or removing and oiling and restitching the big leather drive belts. There's no place to go for spare parts."

The Durgin Bridge (left) over the Swift River, near Tamworth, New Hampshire, completes an icescape worthy of Currier and Ives. In North Conway, New Hampshire, Treffle Bolduc (above) became a terrific—but most unlikely—snowshoe maker. He had been trained as a violinist—a classical musician, not a fiddler of the sort that's popular in other French-speaking families—and was concertmaster for the Manchester, New Hampshire, orchestra when he quit and decided to live by his wits in the woods. He learned snowshoe making from Indians in Quebec and now crafts the shoes by hand in a small shop and sells them all over the world.

The Balsams Hotel (above) in far-northern New Hampshire—note the Canadian as well as American flag— gets the attention of the world every four years when the first votes of the New Hampshire Primary are cast there at midnight and immediately tallied. The grand hotel is located in a town with a colorful name: Dixville Notch, the "Switzerland of the Nation." There are several such notches, or cuts, through the craggy New Hampshire mountains. An old stone portal (opposite) and stone fence (overleaf) are evidence that the Balsams has been in business a long time. It began as the Dix House, a twenty-five-room inn, soon after the Civil War. In 1895 a wealthy Philadelphia inventor, Henry Hale, purchased, renamed, and began to enlarge the hotel. The estate is bigger than Manhattan Island. It offers hiking, mountain biking, fishing, and natural-history programs.

Winter brings special beauty to Vermont's tiny state capital, Montpelier (left), as the capitol dome gleams through the trees, and smoke and mist rise from buildings. Vermont winters inspired poets like Robert Frost. They also mean plenty of activity on mountainsides like Mount Mansfield at Stowe ski resort (above) in the Green Mountains, from which the state gets its name (vert mont). The oldest combination downhill—cross country ski race in the country is held at Stowe each February. Many Vermonters are hardy, outdoors people for whom winter is a time of awakening to outdoor activities, including snowmobiling, snowboarding, snowshoeing, and sleigh rides. They and visitors can even take advantage of an around-the-state cross country skiing adventure that takes them to four country inns along the Catamount Trail.

The public library in Guildhall, Vermont (above), built in 1900, was once a Masonic hall. Guildhall was settled in 1764, ten years after Guildhall Falls was discovered. This remote town in Vermont's "Northern Kingdom" was the frontier during the French and Indian War. One could spend an entire long vacation just visiting and photographing New England steepled churches, like the White Church (opposite), a former Baptist church that is now a community church in Grafton, Vermont. The factors to look for: clean lines, white paint, high steeple, preferably a clear view across a green unobstructed by signs or telephone wires, and unostentatious windows. And there are plenty of small towns for these places of worship that seem to signify New England's humble piety. The state's largest city, Burlington, barely reaches 40,000 population, and Montpelier, at about 8,000, is the nation's smallest capital city.

Unlike her Vanderbilt siblings, Lila Vanderbilt Webb and her husband, William Seward Webb—who ran the Vanderbilts' Wagner Palace Car railroad company—did not turn to Newport, Hyde Park, or the North Carolina mountains to build a country estate. They chose four thousand acres of farmland on Lake Champlain, near the tiny town of Shelburne, Vermont, and built a mansion and model farm. The five-story barn (above) housed a blacksmith shop, workshops, management offices, and stalls for eighty teams of horses. The manor's tea room (right) was used for breakfast and informal dinners. Today Shelburne Farms' Shingle Style manor—imposing by most standards but a mere cottage compared to most Vanderbilt family estates—is a public inn whose profits go to educational endeavors.

A trip to New England is often a search for simple pleasures: a stop by the pond at Windsor (opposite), the "Birthplace of Vermont"; an autumn array outside the Wildflower Inn bed and breakfast in Lyndonville, Vermont (above); a quiet drive down a beautiful road (overleaf) in the Carrabassett Valley of western Maine. Just as Mark Twain wrote that there is "a sumptuous variety about the New England weather that compels the stranger's admiration— and regret," there is a cornucopia of natural wonders to appreciate. The surroundings, like the leaves, can be understated, then fiery. New England is not America's coldest, wettest, highest, or greenest region, and certainly not the wealthiest, but it's a lot of all these things— and the most historic and idiosyncratic. It's a place where the cliché rings true: the more things change, the more they stay the same.

Maine's rocky coast-
line is dotted with
quaint inlets, includ-
ing Northeast Harbor
(left) and Southwest
Harbor (above),
where fishing and
oyster fleets moor
among pleasure boats.
OVERLEAF: Norlands
in Livermore, Maine,
is a working farm and
living-history center
at which visitors leave
behind the vestiges of
twentieth-century life
and, briefly, step into
the arduous world of a
Maine family of 1870.
At Norlands that
family, the Wash-
burns, was a dynasty.
Consider the seven
sons of Israel and
Patty Washburn:
one became governor
of Maine; another
secretary of state
under Ulysses S.
Grant; a third
a U.S. senator from
Minnesota; and the
others, respectively, a
Maine banker, a U.S.
congressman from
Wisconsin, a minister
to Paraguay, and a
U.S. Navy captain.